RAISE *your Vibe*
ROCK *your life!*

111 ways to get you out of your funk and manifesting your dream life

by Elizabeth Bowie

This book is for entertainment purposes only.
Copyright ©, [Elizabeth Bowie], [2022] All rights reserved
Book Design & Published by Aeyshaa
Instagram: aeysha_bookdesign
Paperback ISBN 978-1-915930-95-8
Ebook ISBN 978-1-915930-96-5

Dedicated to the Quirky

Raise your Vibe Rock your life!

CONTENTS

WELCOME ... 6
1. SING ... 11
2. WALK ... 12
3. GARDEN ... 13
4. EPSOM SALT BATH ... 14
5. RING A FRIEND ... 15
6. DANCE ... 16
7. WRITE/PAINT/DRAW ... 17
8. FUNNY MOVIES ... 18
9. MEDICATION ... 19
10. COFFEE ... 20
11. HUM ... 21
12. CHANT ... 22
13. SKIP ... 23
14. READ ... 24
15. THERAPY ... 25
16. MASSAGE ... 26
17. JOURNAL ... 27
18. VISION BOARD ... 28
19. SIT IN THE SUN ... 29
20. MEDITATE ... 30
21. SEX ... 31
22. SELF PLEASURE ... 32
23. COOK ... 33
24. TREE HUGGER ... 34
25. FACE YOUR FEARS ... 35
26. STEP OUTSIDE YOUR COMFORT ZONE ... 36
27. GO ON A DATE ... 37
28. INNER CHILD WORK ... 38
29. PLAY WITH YOUR KIDS ... 39
30. KARAOKE ... 40
31. EAT DESSERT ... 41
32. VOLUNTEER ... 42
33. SET SOCIAL MEDIA BOUNDARIES ... 43
34. GO TO A SHOW ... 44
35. CRYSTALS ... 45
36. SAY FUCK OFF ... 46
37. FORGIVE ... 47
38. EXERCISE ... 48
39. NOURISH YOUR BODY ... 49
40. SPA DAY ... 50
41. PRAY ... 51
42. DATING APPS ... 52
43. HOUSE SHOPPING ... 53
44. DECLUTTER AND ORGANISE ... 54
45. SORT YOUR FINANCES ... 55
46. GET A TATTOO ... 56
47. LEARN SOMETHING NEW ... 57
48. AFFIRMATIONS ... 58
49. QUIT GOSSIPING ... 59
50. RECONNECT ... 60
51. TREAT YOURSELF ... 61
52. SOLO DATE ... 62
53. BUY LINGERIE ... 63

54. DRINK CEREMONIAL CACAO … 64
55. DREAM BIG … 65
56. CULL YOUR CLOTHES … 66
57. TURN OFF THE TV … 67
58. CUT OUT MEAT AND DAIRY … 68
59. SOUND HEALING … 69
60. REIKI … 70
61. STOP PROCRASTINATING … 71
62. TAKE SOME RISKS … 72
63. SIDE HUSTLE … 73
64. HUG … 74
65. ADOPT A RESCUE … 75
66. LOOK AFTER MOTHER EARTH … 76
67. IGNORE THE HATER'S … 77
68. RELEASE YOUR EX … 78
69. NO STALKING … 79
70. MIRROR WORK … 80
71. TRAVEL … 81
72. BE PRESENT … 82
73. GRATITUDE … 83
74. GET A MENTOR … 84
75. DEFINE YOUR VALUES … 85
76. DON'T BE A DOORMAT … 86
77. SAY NO … 87
78. SMILE … 88
79. VISUALISATION … 89
80. LOVE YOURSELF … 90
81. TALK TO A STRANGER … 91
82. MAKE THE FIRST MOVE … 92
83. COMMUNITY … 93
84. HONESTY … 94
85. HAVE FAITH … 95
86. GET HEALTHY … 96
87. SUPPLEMENTS … 97
88. INFRARED SAUNA … 98
89. HYDRATE … 99
90. POOP REGULARLY … 100
91. EAT YOUR GREENS … 101
92. NEVER GIVE UP … 102
93. ADD PLANTS … 103
94. INSPIRED ACTION … 104
95. YOGA … 105
96. SAGE YOUR HOME … 106
97. FULL AND NEW MOON RITUALS … 107
98. EAT CARBS … 108
99. FORGET YOUR AGE … 109
100. CUT CORDS … 110
101. EARTHING … 111
102. MANDALAS … 112
103. SEE A PSYCHIC MEDIUM … 113
104. ESSENTIAL OILS … 114
105. BREATHWORK … 115
106. SWIM IN THE OCEAN … 116
107. PROTEST … 117
108. VISIT A SANCTUARY OR TEMPLE … 118
109. TEA TIME … 119
110. FOREST BATHING … 120
111. SURRENDER … 121

WELCOME

Hello beautiful soul,

I am so glad you have chosen this book or that someone has gifted it to you. I believe we were meant to connect in this small way and I am so bloody happy we have. It brings me great joy to be able to create, inspire and hopefully help others live their best happy and creative lives. I also consider it a privilege and honour, so thank you.

Who am I?

My name is Elizabeth, but most people call me Liz. I have been a working actor, singer and writer for over thirty years and most recently a student of meditation and mindfulness. I grew up in the Eastern Suburbs of Sydney, Australia and after a much-needed tree change, now live in the Blue Mountains, NSW. I am a single mother and have two kids plus a small, neurotic menagerie consisting of a cocker spaniel, three cats, a guinea pig and chooks.

    I teach singing and sing in a few different bands, have several solo music projects on the go, many writing projects and generally consider myself a bit of a rock chick. I love tattoos, pink hair, swearing and lots of loud guitar. I live a reasonably clean lifestyle these days besides a rare G & T, a love of chocolate and my trusty medications. I also have a strong interest in plant-based health, consider myself spiritual, quirky and have perhaps a slightly unhealthy obsession with all things Witchy and Woo-Woo.

    Ever since I was a little girl seeing ghosts in my family home, I have had a fascination with all things Metaphysical -

Manifestation, Law of Attraction, Crystals, Mediums, Psychics, Witches, Spirits and have delved into all of it. I've been ghost hunting, I've participated in covens, I've seen countless mediums and chatted with the dead, I've had shamans come and cleanse my home after a few too many bumps in the night and have filled my home with metaphysical books, crystals and good vibes. However, I actively began to focus more on Manifesting using the Law of Attraction after going through a very long stretch of awfulness, basically life sucked. Let me explain. Over a fifteen-year period, I lost my Mum to cancer, my Dad to dementia, had a miscarriage, got married then divorced and became a single mother struggling to cope financially. I also stopped performing, completely lost my mojo in ALL departments, was diagnosed with an autoimmune disease and my mental health fell apart. It was intense, challenging and exhausting.

By the end of it, I was sick, overweight and completely burnt out. I lost my joy. My love of everything I once felt made up my identity - singing, performing, writing, creating and adventure melted away. I was not myself, at all! I was confused, miserable and didn't know what to do or where to go. It was a very bleak time. What I DID know was that I didn't want to spend the rest of my life in struggle. I wanted to live in joy, laughter, creativity, vibrant health and abundance. So, without even being able to move myself off my couch some days, I started studying and reading all I could get my hands on. I began listening to podcasts and watching videos and absorbing all I could about Manifesting and slowly putting what I learnt into practise. I also began to focus more on my health than I ever had in my life and worked on quieting my mind through meditation and visualisation.

Now I am at best highly cynical, abrupt, opinionated and a classic over sharer, so I don't believe everything I read and don't expect you to either. If it feels good and light it's probably right, if it feels heavy and drab, call it a cab. I say this because I am not the type to have my head in the clouds without at least one foot firmly planted on earth, so I keep it real, but this shit can work, if you allow it too.

Things didn't change overnight for me and are still very much a work in progress. I didn't decide one day I was an expert manifestor and suddenly was living on a beach in Fiji, nor do I have 10 million in the bank (I'm working on it) but I am filled with hope after being so long in the dark, that my life is taking shape in a most beautiful way. I know now to be grateful for all the things I DO have in my life at this very moment. A home that is mine, two beautiful kids I feel blessed to have been able to have, lots of animals to make me laugh, a creative soul that has begun to find her way home, friends who have my back and enough money to live the life we love.

There are countless excellent books on manifesting, and this isn't necessarily one of them, this is more like a pack of angel cards, or guidance cards - you take what you need on a particular day. I decided to write this book as a way of directing my energy and hopefully yours towards bringing all the goodness back into our lives. We really aren't here for long and life flies by, and if you are anything like me, you don't want to waste another second not living the life of your dreams. Or not feeling as good as you have ever felt, reaching those goals, big and small that fill your heart (and your wallet!) I am a fair way through my life now, and I'm not wasting another moment of it, I hope you don't either.

The Key

As I delved into learning about Manifesting and the Law of Attraction, I learnt that it is vital to maintain a vibration that matches the vibration of what you want to attract. For example, if you maintain consistent thoughts such as, 'I never have enough money,' 'I'll never be healthy,' 'Life's shit,' 'Why me?' and so on. It is pretty much guaranteed that that is how your reality will remain, like attracts like. So what am I saying? You can ask the Universe for all you want, but if you don't spend time in the FEELING of already having it, nothing will change.

Here is how you do that. Say for example you want to live in a beautiful home by the ocean (who doesn't right?) Close your eyes, visualise yourself already there, having your morning coffee looking out over the sea, breathe in the salty air, hear the birds sing, see all the beautiful things in your home around you, the people you love with you, now how does that feel? It should feel amazing, sit with that feeling, carry that feeling with you, FEEL as though you already have it, celebrate the joy, be grateful for it, that is the key. Try as you can to keep your vibration high, a match for all the goodness you desire to bring in. Change the way you talk about things, use this book to help you raise your vibe and take daily action steps towards your dream life, then miracles will happen baby!

Gratitude

I know how hard it can be to be grateful for things when life feels like a dumpster fire. I get it. But gratitude is an important part of the manifesting equation. Maybe you don't feel like you have much to be grateful for right now, but you do. It doesn't matter how small or insignificant it feels to you, be grateful. Write it out daily, a short list of three to ten things or more if inspired. Sometimes my list looks like this: I am grateful for my kids, I am grateful for this sunny day, I am grateful for my home, I am grateful for my creativity, I am grateful for this cup of tea and so on. If you put your focus on what IS working, what IS good in your life, more will come.

A Word on Action Steps

Action steps, baby steps or inspired action, whatever you prefer to call it are the little steps you take each day that brings you closer to what you desire. If you want to be a best-selling author, just asking the Universe for that won't make it happen, you actually have to put pen to paper or fingers to keyboard. If you want to lose weight and get healthy, you have to get up off the couch and move your body and eat good food. If you want to have an amazing business, you need to plan it out and take action towards it. Just asking the Universe for what you want is not enough, but if you pair your intentions with action steps and a high vibe, get ready baby.

Think about what it is you want to manifest; now think about a little step you can take towards that goal. I want to release new music this year, so my next action step is to book studio time, then it may be to write new material or some lyrics, or to do some vocal exercises to make sure my voice is in tip top shape. The steps don't have to be big, but they do need to be moving you in the direction of your goal.

Now everyone has bad days, that is completely normal and okay. But try as you can not to stay there for too long, that's where this little book comes in.

How to use this book

Beyond just reading it all from start to finish, try this. If you're having an off day, or just simply want some inspiration on how to raise your energy so you can get busy manifesting the good things, pick up this book and choose an action step. Or you can be a little more playful, close your eyes, ask the Universe what you need for the day and then open up a random page, and there is your answer! This book is meant to be fun, light and a little nudge from the Universe to get you back on track.

I hope it brings you joy.

Have fun sunshine.

Elizabeth

1. SING

> 'The only thing better than singing is more singing.'
> Ella Fitzgerald

> 'Singing is a way of escaping. It's another world. I'm no longer on earth.'
> Edith Piaf

Sing like no one's listening, sing like everyone's listening. You are a superstar, a rock star, a pop star. Giving your vocal cords and lungs a good workout does wonders for your body, your energy and your funky soul. I don't give a damn if you think you sound good or not, it's not the point. Sing in the car, the shower, to your cat, in your partner's ear. You are doing this to stir up that stagnant energy and to bring joy into your heart and who knows, you may discover a hidden voice you never dared let out. Let go of other people's opinions, you have the right to creative expression starting with using your voice. Create a play list of all the tunes that make you feel awesome and that you enjoy belting along too, then get your inner diva on, raise those endorphins and crank it out!

2. WALK

> 'The walking of which I speak has nothing in it akin to taking exercise, as it is called, as the sick take medicine at stated hours ...but it is itself the enterprise and adventure of the day.'
> Henry David Thoreau

> 'Walking is a man's best medicine.'
> Hippocrates

I'm not a fan of exercise, in fact I loathe it, I am really quite a lazy person but walking for me is different. Walking can be a gentle meditation that is also excellent for your body and mental health. Get outside, walk barefoot on the sand, by the ocean, the lake, follow the bush track, explore your neighbourhood, whatever works. Use the treadmill that is currently a clothes rack. Listen to your favourite playlist, podcast as you walk, or as I often do, listen to the sounds around you, be present and acknowledge all the things you are grateful for, that are currently in your life and that are to come. Movement is essential for shifting stagnant energy so pull on your trainers and get going. Get the Vitamin D on your skin and your heart pumping. Your body and mind will thank you.

3. GARDEN

> ❝
>
> *'I just think that gardening is about the future, a slow thing, that is deep and spiritual as well as spiritually rewarding.'*
> *Monty Don*

Get your hands in the dirt, feel the earth and connect. Gardening is well known for helping people with their mental health, there is something so nourishing about directly connecting with the earth in this way. Your stress will drain out of you and away into the earth. It will ground you, calm your nervous system and you'll get exercise and the satisfaction of being productive. Grow your own food and you'll have the added health benefits and pleasure of eating home grown, freshly picked organic food. All you need is a few pots if you don't have a big backyard, honestly, homegrown tomatoes are next level delicious. Grow your own herbs for cooking, it will save you money and make your food tasty. Grow pretty flowers, add splashes of colour to your environment and feel your soul lift. Make your garden a little haven you can retreat too, make it a peaceful and happy place for you and most importantly, get those hands dirty!

4. EPSOM SALT BATH

> 'She makes use of the soft of the bread for a napkin. She falls asleep at times with shoes on, on unmade beds. When a little money comes in, June buys delicacies, strawberries in the winter, caviar and bath salts.'
> Anais Nin

Having an Epsom salt bath is an excellent way to cleanse yourself, detox, relax and absorb some magnesium. If you have tight, sore muscles soak in a bath for about twenty minutes. Salt is also excellent for cleansing away all the yucky negativity of the day and helping you to reset. Listen to some beautiful music as you soak or read a few chapters of an inspiring and uplifting book, or just close those peepers and let go. Adding a few drops of your favourite essential oil (suitable for skin contact), or non-toxic bubble bath is an extra, delicious treat. Light your favourite candle and say goodbye to all the negativity and stagnant energy. All you have to do is lay there, it's perfect. Sip your favourite wine, kombucha, or sparkling water and cleanse away!

5. RING A FRIEND

> *'If you have two friends in your lifetime, you're lucky. If you have one good friend, you're more than lucky.'*
> S.E Hinton

A good friend that is, one that lifts you up and supports you. Not the friend who unloads all their drama and bitches about life's misery without taking a single step to change a thing. Those sneaky energy vampires, you know the ones, those who need to one up your current issues with their own, you don't need that right now, you are on a mission to reach the stars baby! I'm not saying don't be there for someone you hold dearly, but set your boundaries, don't buy into gossip or bitchiness. That will bring your vibration crashing down and you are better than that, way better. You are a fucking Rockstar remember? Inspire and support each other, have a bloody good laugh, fill each other's cups and feel your energy soar.

6. DANCE

> *'And those who were seen dancing were thought to be insane by those who could not hear the music.'*
> Friedrich Nietzsche

> *'You dance love, and you dance joy, and you dance dreams.'*
> Gene Kelly

Next to walking this is my favourite way to move my body. Move YOUR body and get your freak on, get weird. Dance like Napoleon Dynamite, dance like Lady Gaga or Tina Turner. Dance like you've never danced before. Get sexy, get dorky, get silly, get moving. Put on some music that lights up your soul: rock, pop, disco, country, death metal, throat singing, who cares, whatever works for you. Or chuck on some chanting/mantra music and get your spiritual self vibing. Join a Zumba class, follow some You Tube dance classes, there are so many options. Do not worry about how you look, do not judge, do not care, just dance. Get moving Queen!

7. WRITE/PAINT/DRAW

> 'Lock up your libraries if you like; but there is no gate, no lock, no bolt that you can set upon the freedom of my mind.'
> Virginia Woolf

> 'We write to taste life twice, in the moment and in retrospect.'
> Anais Nin

Stoke your creative juices and do some writing. Make up some stories or write the story of your life. Creative fiction or creative non-fiction, some sci fi, romance, horror, crime, comedy, whatever floats your boat. Maybe you have a screenplay in you, write it. Head to your local café, order your favourite coffee or tea and put some words down. Don't judge it, the goal isn't to be perfect or even published and don't edit as you go, just keep typing or writing. This is just for you. No one ever has to see it, unless you want them too. Let yourself go. If writing isn't your bag, bring out the paints, the charcoals, the pastels, the pencils, whatever medium you prefer and create. You can get affordable canvases from discount stores or a sketch book if you prefer. I am not an artist, I can't draw or paint very well at all, but it doesn't stop me from doing it if that's what I'm 'drawn' to in that moment. Expressing yourself creatively is one of the best ways to raise your vibe and to bring inspiration back into your life. Give it a go.

8. FUNNY MOVIES

> *'A day without laughter is a day wasted.'*
> *Charlie Chaplin*

Make some popcorn, get some Lolly Gobble Bliss Bombs, grab a wine or drink of choice, chuck on one of your favourite comedies and laugh. 'Laughter is the best medicine,' right? Who said that? Laughing raises your vibe, makes you happy and shakes away any shitty feelings you have lurking. Laughing with someone else is even better. Laugh till the tears stream down your face, laugh until you pee yourself. Mums, you know what I'm saying! I love some Schitt's Creek or The Office for a quick bite of comedy, but you do you. Maybe Bridesmaids or Black Adder? You know your sense of humour, curl up with your favourite human or your furbaby and get your giggles on.

9. MEDICATION

> *'I'm just broken. But in a way that makes me ... me. My drugs don't define me. I'm not psychotic. I'm not dangerous. The drugs I take are just a pinch of salt. A little seasoning in life, if you will.'*
> Jenny Lawson

Sometimes medication is one of the stepping stones needed to help you get your groove back. There is absolutely no shame using medication and absolutely necessary in many cases. I myself have been on and off medication most of my adult life and I am fine with that. It has saved me many times and helped me keep my head above water so I can begin to do some of the other things that will help me feel better. You use what you can to get where you want to go. (Without harming others of course!) If you think this is what you may need, reach out to your Doctor and have an honest discussion. You can do ALL the things to raise your vibe but if you currently have a mental illness, perhaps you need a little extra support to help get you there, you deserve to be looked after, you deserve to put yourself first. Get the help you need gorgeous one.

10. COFFEE

> 'Even bad coffee is better than no coffee at all.'
> David Lynch

This is a no brainer, if you want an instant perk, an instant lift me up, have a cup of joe. I love a morning coffee, but I tend to stop at one or at the very least I won't have one after midday as it disrupts my sleep and makes me jitterish. If you are feeling too anxious, it is usually best to give this one a miss. If you crash too hard after, also give it a miss but if not, sip away on some fine organic brew with a yummy plant-based milk. Ditch the sugar though.

11. HUM

> *'There are millions of neurons in the brain. Humming Om chanting create resonance patterns between different brain regions that foster subsequent long-term plasticity changes in the brain.'*
> Amit Ray

Do what now? Trust me on this. Not only is humming an excellent way to warm up a voice for singing and speaking, it is also extremely calming. Humming is self-soothing, it helps your nervous system regulate therefore reducing stress and chilling you out. You don't need any special skills to hum, you don't need a 'good' voice, you just need to hum. If you'd like to take it a step further, you could try chanting. 'OM' is basically a hum and to oversimplify its meaning, it is considered to be the Sound of the Universe.

So gently hum each day, hum along to a song you like, close your eyes and hum, play around with pitch, have fun, you can only feel better.

12. CHANT

> *'One of the main differences between silent meditation and chanting is that silent meditation is rather dependent on concentration, but when you chant, it's more of a direct connection with God.'*
> *George Harrison*

There are so many different chants, if it is all new to you, perhaps listen to some chanting meditations and pick up on some chants that resonate with you. You could do a simple 'OM' (pronounced AH-UU-MM) as mentioned before or one of my favourites, 'OM MANI PADME HUM' a Mantra based in Buddhist tradition which according to the Dalai Lama means to 'Transform your impure body, speech and mind into the pure body, speech and mind of a Buddha.' You don't need to be sitting on a mountain top in lotus position to chant, you don't need to say it perfectly either, you just need to give it a go. If you have a mala or prayer beads you can count your chants along with each bead. There are usually 108 beads, so you say the chant of your choice 108 times as you move through each bead. It is a meditation, it is time for you to relax and refocus and let go.

13. SKIP

> *'I still get wildly enthusiastic about little things...I play with leaves, I skip down the street and run against the wind.'*
> *Leo Buscaglia*

Hello inner child, are you in there? Let's connect, you remember how to skip, let's do it because it's fun. Do it because it reminds you to not take life so seriously, it helps you to remember you were once a kid. That kid (or inner child) is still in you wanting to connect, to be played with, to be allowed to come out and shine. Don't worry if people stare, maybe they will join in? Maybe you just gave them permission to let some joy into their lives. It is also an excellent way to get fit, not that that is the point here. So grab a rope if you like and skip or even better, hold someone's hand and skip down the street. Skip to it!

14. READ

> "From the moment I picked up your book until I put it down, I was convulsed with laughter. Someday I intend reading it."
> Groucho Marx

I love a good book, even an average one to be fair. Reading inspirational, motivational books each day, or listening to podcasts/audio books, is one sure way to get your manifesting mojo running. But you don't need to limit yourself to non-fiction, there are so many amazing, uplifting creative stories waiting to be shared. Set yourself a little time each day to read a few pages, perhaps in bed before you go to sleep, that's my favourite time. Fall asleep with positive thoughts in your mind and good vibes in your soul. Some of my favourites include, Eat, Pray Love ~ Elizabeth Gilbert. The Alchemist ~ Paulo Coelho,

The Happiest Man on Earth ~ Eddie Jaku and The Midnight Library ~ Matt Haig. But the list is endless, find what resonates, what makes you feel happy and tingly and read on.

15. THERAPY

> *'Sadly, too often, the stigma around mental health prevents people who need help from seeking it. But that simply doesn't make any sense. Whether and illness affects your heart, your arm, or your brain, it's still and illness, and there shouldn't be any distinction. We should make it clear that getting help isn't a sign of weakness.'*
> Michelle Obama

I have had a tonne of therapy in my life and mostly it has been very helpful. You just need to make sure you find the right therapist who you really can relax with. It might take a few tries, but don't give up. Having someone to check in with on a regular basis can be extremely beneficial and can help to clear some blocks, negative thought patterns and behaviours. Depending what country you live in, there may be Government support to help cover the cost of sessions. In Australia, you can access a Mental Health Care plan which gives you a certain amount of sessions a year at a heavily discounted rate. If you can access support and feel you could benefit then do, but I realise this isn't an affordable option for everyone. But if you can access it, go for it and as Michelle says, feel no shame, you are bloody smart taking care of your brain the way you would the rest of your body.

16. MASSAGE

> *'The way to health is to have an aromatic bath and a scented massage every day.'*
> *Hippocrates*

I am a huge fan of massage. I know some people don't like being touched, but if you do, then massage is for you. I could have one daily, that would be heaven. I don't have them often enough, but when I do I melt. I even love it when they work those nasty knots out. Bliss! There are also so many different types of massage, you are bound to find one that suits. Swedish, remedial, hot stone, aromatherapy, shiatsu ~ you'll find one you like. Like all health care providers, search around until you find one that works for you, get recommendations, after all they are touching your body and that is sacred. Our local women's health centre has an option to book in for very reasonably priced massages and they are damn good. Often massage students' need bodies to practise is so that is an excellent option if you are watching your budget. Find a massage therapist that works for you and treat yourself when you can because you deserve it.

17. JOURNAL

> *'Fill your paper with the breathings of your heart.'*
> William Wordsworth

Starting each day or ending it (or both) with journaling is a brilliant way to clear the mental clutter, organise your thoughts, set intentions and to write out your gratitude. You would do well to incorporate journaling into your daily spiritual practice. Go and get yourself a beautiful journal and a lush pen that you love to write with, get comfy and get it all out on the page. There is something so beautiful about writing on paper in this way but if you love your technology, a computer is just as good. Just as long as you are clearing your thoughts, thus opening the door to guidance and revelations along the way. Take a deep breath, then put pen to paper. Amazing insights may come to you when you develop this practise, at the very least it will help you destress by not carrying around all the thoughts you have now released onto the page.

18. VISION BOARD

> 'Creating a vision board is probably one of the most valuable visualization tools available to you." And that's because vision boards work.'
> Jack Canfield

This one has me all excited, I LOVE a good vision board. It is one of the most fun and creative ways to let the Universe know exactly what you want to manifest. Get some magazines and cut out pictures of what you desire. Stick them to a board of your choosing. Remember not to attach to the actual things but to the feeling they give you when you see them, it is the feeling that raises your vibration and brings you ever closer to manifesting what you desire. You may prefer to put all your pictures in a scrapbook or if you prefer going paper free, Pinterest is also fabulous to use. I do all three. Make it pretty, add some sparkle, some affirmations or whatever floats your boat. Then get to work, start taking baby steps to achieve the things you have on that board. You can't just stick pictures up and sit back waiting for the knock on the door, you must take inspired action to move towards those things. The Universe will meet you half way.

19. SIT IN THE SUN

> 'The late afternoon sunlight, warm as oil, sweet as childhood ...'
> Stephen King

Soak in those nourishing, warming rays. Start each day with some sunlight on your face and skin, it helps regulate your hormones therefore helping you sleep. Get your vitamin D for the day and let those blissful vibes fill your body. Close your eyes, feel the warmth on your face, take a deep breath and relax. Maybe lay on a picnic blanket with your favourite book and have some 'you' time. Just remember, if in Australia or a similar climate, avoid midday when the sun is at its hottest. But otherwise, it's free and delicious, enjoy it.

20. MEDITATE

> *'Our thoughts are not roadblocks to our meditation, they are the divine expression of the universe and the building blocks of infinite possibilities available to us in every moment.'*
> *David Ji*

This is a must. No argument. Do it. Got it? Great! Now let me elaborate. You don't have to be sitting lotus style on a cushion letting your knees ache and your butt go numb. You can walk, dance, garden, colour, chant, cook, swim, run, listen to music, anything where you leave all the stress and monkey mind behind and just be. There are loads of apps that do guided mediations too, Insight Timer is the one I mostly use and that I also am a teacher on. You can select a theme and time length for your meditation and settle in. Or take a moment now, and just sit and observe your breath, watch it as it moves in and out, don't control it, just observe. When your mind wanders, gently bring your attention back to your breath, is it shallow or deep in your belly? Are you breathing fast or slow? Just slowing down and observing is all you need to do. There are so many ways to meditate and so many teachers. One of my favourite teachers is Davidji, he is brilliant, warm and wonderful. Check him out if you like. As always find what resonates for you and get stuck in. Along with journaling, make this part of your daily practise.

21. SEX

> *'It's not true that I had nothing on. I had the radio on.'*
> *Marilyn Monroe*

I'm talking consensual, mutually pleasurable, mind blowing sex. Sex where you feel like the beautiful, sexy, diva goddess that you are. Your pleasure and orgasms are your divine right, embrace them and rock them. Women are so often shamed if they express enjoyment of sex, it has, in the past, been thought of as something for men to enjoy, and we are there to make sure 'they' get off. No more ladies, whatever kind of sex you're having, with whatever gender or non-binary soul, rock it, enjoy it and feel your vibration rise. No pun intended but toys are a great addition too!

22. SELF PLEASURE

"

'Good sex is like good bridge. If you don't have a good partner, you'd better have a good hand.'
Mae West

A bit cheeky to some but honestly, you know your body better than anyone and there is no shame in exploring, relishing and getting yourself off. Your 'vibe' will be sky high after an awesome orgasm. Add some toys to the mix, explore and enjoy. You do not need another to have physical pleasure. Sometimes it's better on your own! I know you hear me ladies. Also, the more you know your own body and what you like, the more you can help partners learn how to rock your world. Highly recommend.

23. COOK

> *'Cooking is at once child's play and adult joy. And cooking done with care is an act of love.'*
> Craig Claiborne

Sometimes, when you don't have to cook every meal that gets eaten in your home, like I do, cooking can be a pleasurable thing. It's creative and inspiring for all the senses. Follow a recipe if that's your thing, or just experiment. Make something utterly delicious and eat it with mindfulness, savouring every bite. As you cook, put on some music you love, sip your wine, or water and immerse yourself in the experience and honestly if it doesn't end up tasting great, who gives a fuck. Either eat it, or order a pizza, you still had fun.

24. TREE HUGGER

> *'Never say there is nothing beautiful in the world anymore. There is always something to make you wonder in the shape of a tree, the trembling of a leaf.'*
> Albert Schweitzer

I LOVE hugging trees and consider myself a proud tree hugger. Trees are made up of energy just like us, trees literally give us life. We would not exist without them so show them some love. Hug one, say thank you, or sit under one and read, meditate, chillout, have a picnic. Get your full hippy on and be one with trees. Have a chat, tell it your worries and let them go. Listen to its leaves rustling in response, feel its energy. Do what you can to nurture trees and protect them. If you have some land plant some trees, or join environmental groups and do forest restoration, park restoration or anything that places more trees in the earth.

25. FACE YOUR FEARS

> 'Facing it, always facing it, that's the way to get through. Face it.'
> Conrad Joseph

> 'A life lived in fear is a life half lived.'
> Strictly Ballroom

Hiding away and avoiding things that you fear will only make the fear intensify. Scared of public speaking? Join toastmasters. Hate going out alone? Have a coffee by yourself at your local café. For me even making phone calls can be terrifying, so I have to push myself. It can be exhilarating to do something you have always avoided because of fear. You will feel proud of yourself and perhaps be more confident to push the envelope a little further each time. Have faith in yourself. Go as big or small as you want, just challenge yourself. You can do it!

26. STEP OUTSIDE YOUR COMFORT ZONE

> *'The further you get away from yourself, the more challenging it is. Not to be in your comfort zone is great fun.'*
> Benedict Cumberbatch

Similar to facing your fears but perhaps not as intense? Are you nice and snug inside your routine, blissfully happy in doing the same thing or do you have a feeling that there is more to life? If so, why not try doing one thing each day that pushes you just a little outside your comfort zone. It doesn't have to be a big deal, maybe it's cooking a meal you wouldn't normally try, returning a phone call when you loathe talking on the phone (okay as I said before, phone calls can be hard!) Saying hello to a stranger as you pass them on the street, they may think you odd, but that's half the fun, wearing a colour you normally avoid, saying no to something when you always say yes. You know what's right for you.

27. GO ON A DATE

> 'Let's start with this statistic: You are delicious. Be brave, my sweet. I know you can get lonely. I know you can crave companionship and sex and love so badly that it physically hurts. But I truly believe that the only way you can find out that there's something better out there is to first believe there's something better out there. What other choice is there?'
> Greg Behrendt

Hey singles! If you are reading this sitting in an Oodie with Netflix on in the background, (not that there is anything wrong with that. I'm sitting here in mine) it's time to step out. Go on date. It doesn't have to be 'The One' it can just be a cup of coffee and a nice chat. It is more about seeing what's out there, shaking up your energy to get things moving. Of course, if you'd rather eat chalk than go on another date, skip the other person and take yourself out to dinner. This will also shift things around energetically, you just can't lose. And you might meet someone unexpectedly? The Universe has a multitude of tricks up its sleeve. Go for it.

28. INNER CHILD WORK

> *'The most sophisticated people I know - inside they are all children.'*
> *Jim Henson*

Next time you are admonishing yourself, next time you are putting yourself down, hating on yourself stop and think, would I say this stuff to my own child? To my niece/nephew, or to a small innocent child figuring the world out? No of course you wouldn't, or if you would, then you need to figure out what that's about. Your inner child is listening, you have to embrace that child, give love not criticism. Start to repair the hurts, start to heal yourself. Get a picture of yourself as a child and tell yourself while looking at it that you love them, you are there for them, you will from this moment on keep them safe. My God, you are so wonderful, start treating yourself as such. Give the mini you lots of love and mental hugs. The healing will be mind blowing.

29. PLAY WITH YOUR KIDS

> 'It is a happy talent to know how to play.'
> Ralph Waldo Emerson

Your kids want to spend time with you, find pockets of time where you can unleash your inner child and play with your kids, the sillier the better. They will love connecting with you, my kids always wanted to play and that is starting to change a little now they are growing up so I am soaking it up before they are surly teenagers that want nothing more to do with me. Make fun of yourself, make them laugh, find the joy in being playful. Don't be concerned about looking silly. Play board games, elastics, twister, Super Mario, throw on VR headset, whatever it is. Just connect.

30. KARAOKE

> 'Some may say that I couldn't sing, but no one can say that I didn't sing.'
> Florence Foster Jenkins

I have already told you how awesome singing is for you so why not step it up a notch? Gather some friends and put on your own mini show. Now you'll have laughter, duets, cocktails and mocktails and some serious healing and vibe raising if you let yourself feel free and let go. The first time I ever did karaoke, someone chose Amazing Grace for me to sing, now it's a great tune but so serious and it felt more like a performance than a fun way to blow off steam and have fun. So now I will ALWAYS choose music that makes me want to dance and brings me joy. Do not take yourself seriously, the more ridiculous the better. Go karaoke queens!

31. EAT DESSERT

> *'Then I went for a walk and ate some pistachio gelato. Which Italians consider a perfectly reasonable thing to be eating at 9:30 a.m. and frankly I could not agree with them more.'*
> *Elizabeth Gilbert*

Life is too short to say no to things that bring you pleasure. I'm not saying go to Woolies, buy a cheesecake and eat the whole thing in front of the TV, although if you want to, who am I to judge? What I am saying is, allow yourself the pleasure of eating the delicious dessert, the piece of cake at the office party, the bit of chocolate after dinner, the packet of biscuits when you have your period (we've all been there) Don't judge yourself for doing so, if you're eating nourishing healthy food most of the time and having respect for your body then you'll be just fine. There are also plenty of options for those of us with food intolerances and allergies. I got a delicious gluten and dairy free cheesecake from the supermarket recently and no I didn't eat it all myself, but hey if I could have if I wanted. YUM.

32. VOLUNTEER

> 'The best way to not feel hopeless is to get up and do something. Don't wait for good things to happen to you. If you go out and make some good things happen, you will fill the world with hope, you will fill yourself with hope.'
> Barak Obama

Helping others is souls work isn't it? You will feel fulfilled and warm and fuzzy inside. And you are doing a bloody good thing. I have done lots of volunteering for animal welfare organisations, and also mentoring for teens. It fills my heart to be of service and will fill yours too. So, make a difference, choose something that resonates with you and get out there. Maybe you want to volunteer at an op-shop, a soup kitchen, an animal shelter, reading at a library? Whatever it is, do it. Bonus karma points may apply too.

33. SET SOCIAL MEDIA BOUNDARIES

❝

'Social media gives legions of idiots the right to speak when they once only spoke at a bar after a glass of wine, without harming the community ... but now they have the same right to speak as a Nobel Prize winner. It's the invasion of the idiots.'
Umberto Eco

'Distracted from distraction by distraction.'
T.S Eliot

I love social media, most of the time. But there is a stinky side to it too. If you are wasting too much time endlessly scrolling, comparing, and feeling shit about yourself, it might just be the time to cut back. Unfollow anyone that makes you feel bad about yourself. Set time limits on yourself or just check once or twice a day. If it is really toxic in your life, ditch it. You are too fucking fabulous to have your vibe crushed by anything or anyone. I know, easier said than done, phone addiction is real, but it eats up a lot of time and if you want to crush it in life and be the sensational goddess you are, you must set your priorities and scrolling isn't one of them. Now if you are experiencing any sort of bullying or trolling know that most people do as they rise to their full potential, live their truth and become more successful. This does not make it okay, but also know that the trolls are often sad, misguided, lost people filled with hate for themselves hiding behind a keyboard. Block, delete, report, move on.

34. GO TO A SHOW

> *'All the world's a stage,*
> *And all the men and women merely players;*
> *They have their exits and their entrances,*
> *And one man in his time plays many parts.'*
> William Shakespeare

Do you love Theatre? Musicals? Opera? Live Music? Go along and see a show or get to a gig. There is something so thrilling about seeing a live show. Immerse yourself in the story, in the imaginary world the actors and singers are bringing to life. Dance along or head bang to the music from a band you love or discover a new band. As Eminem says,

'You better - lose yourself in the music, the moment

You own it, you better never let it go

You only get one shot, do not miss your chance to blow

This opportunity comes once in a lifetime'

I get a thrill after a great performance or super fun gig, I feel inspired and energised, and if this is your bag, I imagine you will too.

35. CRYSTALS

> *'In a crystal we have clear evidence of the existence of a formative life principle, and though we cannot understand the life of a crystal, it is nonetheless a living being.'*
> Nicola Tesla

I love me a lot of Woo-Woo and you don't get much more Woo-Woo than crystals. There are plenty of online guides and books available that outline what each crystal is best for, but I would suggest firstly using your intuition to guide you to what you may need. Start with what you are drawn too and go from there. Trust the Universe that you are choosing the right ones, they are all amazing and all have benefits. Give them a little cleanse with some sage when you first get them and also pop them out under each full moon to cleanse and charge them with delicious moon energy. Wear them as jewellery, stick them in your bra or pockets, under your pillows, around your home, the opportunities are endless.

36. SAY FUCK OFF

> *'A lot of people lacked that gift: knowing when to fuck off.'*
> Gillian Flynn

Simple and effective. If there is someone being toxic in your life, send them (with love) off on their merry fucking way. You have no time for these people. Now I'm being a little cheeky telling you to say fuck off, and I don't mean get up in their face and do so, that's not good for your vibes at all. But what I do mean is, you can scream it off a mountain, under a bridge as a train passes by, into your pillow, just let it out and send all the bad energy and people away out of your life. I must admit that Fuck is one of my favourite swear words that I use daily. So, yell it with me, FUCK OFF!

37. FORGIVE

> *'Always forgive your enemies;
> nothing annoys them so much.'*
> Oscar Wilde

Forgiveness is extremely powerful and necessary for you to clear energetic sludge and to move on in your life with joy and manifesting power. Forgiving others but also forgiving yourself. Forgiving myself for a lot of the decisions I have made in my life has been a monumental task. But if I continued to beat myself up about my choices and carry the guilt and shame of these decisions, my life would just continue to be a stagnant pool of misery (Fun right?) I have worked very hard to forgive myself and release guilt and shame, and also just as hard at forgiving others. I have forgiven abuse, mistreatment, unkindness, unfairness, bullying, and so on. I haven't forgotten and would never accept being treated this way again, but I have forgiven. Think about people you need to forgive, even without an apology, set yourself free, cut the cord that links you to them and then forgive yourself. Look into a mirror, into your own eyes and say, 'I forgive you and I love you.' Say it as many times as you need too. Tears are ok, it is clearing and healing. You've got this beautiful.

38. EXERCISE

> 'All truly great thoughts are conceived while walking.'
> Friedrich Nietzsche
>
> 'An early-morning walk is a blessing for the whole day.'
> Henry David Thoreau

This is vital. You know I don't love it, but for Goddesses sake, find something you actually like doing, you don't have to love it but at least like it. For example, I love dancing, don't mind yoga and walking. I have graced the occasional Zumba class, which is absolutely fun and a good workout, or I'll throw on some music and dance around my home and get my heart pumping. You can get free yoga online, my favourite is Yoga with Adrienne and walking is free too. Maybe the gym is your thing, get up and go. Whatever it is, just do it. Your body, your confidence, your mental health, your manifesting vibes will thank you big time.

39. NOURISH YOUR BODY

> *'If we could give every individual the right amount of nourishment and exercise, not too little and not too much, we would have found the safest way to health.'*
> Hippocrates

Feed your body high vibe, healthy, fresh food. Limit or fuck off completely food that brings your vibration down. Processed foods, dead foods, sugar, chemicals, food with ingredients you don't understand, foods with more than a few ingredients. Get it out of your cupboards, get it out of your trolleys, and most importantly get it out of your body. This shit will break you down, mess with your cells and grime up your energy. Instead, incorporate fresh fruit, a rainbow of vegetables, loads of leafy greens, flaxseed or chia (get the bowels moving) lots of water, legumes, beans, nuts and so on. Drink lots of water, experiment with recipes, add some medicinal mushrooms, make some yummy salads, eat what works for your body, discard what doesn't. If you can afford it, go organic when you can. Spending a little more now will save you in medical bills in the long run. You are worth it, you deserve to look after yourself. You are adored.

40. SPA DAY

> *'If we do not know how to take care of ourselves and to love ourselves, we cannot take care of the people we love. Loving oneself is the foundation for loving another person.'*
> *Thich Nhat Hanh*

Hey you! Divine goddess, you deserve to take time out and be pampered. Go get a facial, your hair done, a massage, a mani/pedi, whatever it is that you enjoy. Shake things up, move that energy. Have you had the same haircut and colour since 1995? Change it. (Unless you're Lisa Rinna) If finances are a concern, DIY can be just as good. Get some friends around and make a day of it, facemasks can be made from ingredients you have in your cupboard. Organic, non-toxic hair colour is in most supermarkets, order some gorgeous nail colours. Put on some tunes, chill out and glam up.

41. PRAY

> *'You pray in your distress and in your need; would that you might pray also in the fullness of your joy and in your days of abundance.'*
> Kahill Gibran

You don't need to be religious to benefit from prayer, you can pray to whomever or whatever you believe. I pray to The Universe, my guides, guardian angels, source and sometimes God. But God to me is not a white man with a beard sitting up there making rules and judging us. God is the energy of the Universe and we are all God. You don't need to go to a church, although you can if that's your thing. You don't need to kneel by your bed. You can speak to the Universe anywhere and anytime. You can pray about anything, it is more about feeling a connection to something greater than yourself. It helps me not feel so alone at times, it helps me find clarity and to heal. Praying can be a very soothing practice, maybe give it a try.

42. DATING APPS

> *'It's not Great Cupid or even Good Cupid. It's Ok Cupid.'*
> Helen Hong

Have you been on dating apps for ages and keep seeing the same men recycled, pics of men holding fish, shirtless in the bathroom, selfies at the gym or the worst of all, photos with their kids? Maybe it's time to have a break. Spend some time nourishing the Goddess you are, the more radiant you are and the more you own your power, the better a partner you'll attract. Now I can only speak from my own limited experience and that is primarily looking at men on these apps, but I have always ending up deleting it before even meeting anyone as I am left so uninspired. I also feel my energy drain as I swipe through hundreds of people, it isn't a good feeling and brings my vibe way down. Now if all that hasn't turned you off and you're NOT on dating apps, sure go on have a peek, you never know your luck. I know loads of people have met their partners online, especially these days. It can be nice to have a chat and maybe a coffee or maybe more. But the minute it feels like shit, fuck it off.

43. HOUSE SHOPPING

> *'Create the highest, grandest vision possible for your life, because you become what you believe.'*
> Oprah Winfrey

If your dream board is filled with images of gorgeous houses, take yourself to some open days and check out houses like the ones you see yourself living in. Feel yourself living there as you wander around, align with being deserving, align with the energy of the home. Don't limit yourself either, if you want to live in a mansion, go check them out, if you want a small cottage by the sea, go to them. The sooner you align and feel deserving of living in such a way, combined with inspired action the sooner these things can come into your orbit. And don't worry about the fact you aren't really there to buy, just smile and pretend you are, because one day you will be!

44. DECLUTTER AND ORGANISE

> *'No matter how wonderful things used to be, we cannot live in the past. The joy and excitement we feel here and now are more important.'*
> Marie Kondo

If you live in a cluttered environment, it will be hard to achieve a calm sense of mind. I know I get anxious surrounded by mess and clutter and that I feel amazing after a good clean up and declutter session. Simplicity is key. Marie Kondo your stuff, although I'd keep the books. Make space in your home, clear out stagnant energy, go room to room decluttering and cleaning. Organise and donate. If you want to attract a partner, clear out a drawer for them, let the Universe know what you want. Make your home peaceful, clean and clear of mess. Be ruthless, don't hang onto stuff 'just in case.' Your home is meant to be your haven. Once you've done this, burn some sage, open the windows and let the negative energy out, say a little prayer, something like,

'I say goodbye to all negative energy and let in light, love and peace.'

Light some candles and enjoy your beautiful, peaceful space.

45. SORT YOUR FINANCES

> 'Never ask of money spent Where the spender thinks it went. Nobody was ever meant To remember or invent What he did with every cent.'
> Robert Frost

I followed Frost's advice for most of my life but now I operate a little differently. Pay your bills on time, pay off debt, don't have debt collectors messing with your vibe. Get a side hustle, work more hours, make him finally pay the child support, whatever you need to do to clear your financial woes. I would even suggest getting rid of your credit cards, I haven't had one in years and if I want to buy something outside my budget now, there are always services like Afterpay. But be wary, you can get into trouble using these services and late fees apply, so if you have trouble staying on top of spending, don't sign up. Control what you spend, track it, budget, only buy what you need until you are clear of debt. Put a little aside in an emergency fund for peace of mind, put a little in savings. If you know you have some money to fall back on, the feeling of lack will dissipate, and more money will energetically be allowed into your life. Having some cash in the bank will give you a sense of security and take away the panic if something breaks, or an unexpected bill crops up. Get some easy to follow financial books, The Barefoot Investor has a couple and I find them very useful and easy-peasy to follow, but there are so many. The point is, as long as you have financial issues, you will never feel at peace. Make sorting your finances a priority. Get professional advice. Just don't give up your morning coffee, everyone needs some joy!

46. GET A TATTOO

> *'I am a canvas of my experiences, my story is etched in lines and shading, and you can read it on my arms, my legs, my shoulders, and my stomach.'*
> Kat Von D

I know this is not for everyone, but I am a tattoo junkie. I love them, good ones that is. Some of mine are shitty but they are mine and remind me of different times in my life. Get a tattoo that reminds you of a brilliant time in your life, a reminder of your beliefs, something that motivates you, or just because it is damn gorgeous. Nothing wrong with that. Find a recommended artist and be fussy, get exactly what you want and if the vibe is off, keep searching for someone else. Seeing some art on your body that you love each day will put smile on your face and if tattoos are just not your vibe, you can always play with temporary ones for a little fun.

47. LEARN SOMETHING NEW

> *'I am always doing that which I cannot do, in order that I may learn how to do it.'*
> Pablo Picasso

Is there something you have you always wanted to do and learn but have put off time and time again? A new language, salsa dancing, pottery, cooking, writing, singing, drawing, skiing, coding, yodelling? Don't put it off, stimulate your brain and your creativity. You never know what might happen and who you might meet stepping outside your comfort zone and embracing something new, plus your brain will love you for it. Keep challenging yourself, keep evolving, don't get stagnant on me baby.

48. AFFIRMATIONS

> *'You have the power to heal your life, and you need to know that. We think so often that we are helpless, but we're not. We always have the power of our minds...Claim and consciously use your power.'*
> *'Every thought we think is creating our future.'*
> Louise Hay

Louise Hay was the goddess who introduced me (and the world) to the concept of affirmations. Her book 'You can heal your life,' was a game changer. Now they are commonly used to reset your mindset and elevate your energy and thoughts. There are so many ways to use affirmations, you can write them on post it notes and put them around your environment, say them into a mirror, sing them, pull affirmation cards, listen to affirmation meditations. The list is endless. Just add them to your daily routine and watch your life and mood elevate. You can start simply, just say one each morning on rising, maybe

'I am worthy,' 'Today will be a good day,' 'Money comes to me easily,' or my fav, 'The kids will do what I ask of them today.' Okay, who am I kidding....

49. QUIT GOSSIPING

> *'Strong minds discuss ideas, average minds discuss events, weak minds discuss people.'*
> Socrates

Gossiping about others is a nasty, low vibe way to waste your precious time. I have been guilty of it for sure, it can be low-vibe entertainment but only if you want to stay in a negative and non-manifesting place. Stop spreading it and stop listening to it. Raise people up, don't tear them down. I imagine once you set this boundary, the gossip loving people in your life will kick back and react but the more you stay in integrity, the more you will attract the right people into your life. Lead with love baby.

50. RECONNECT

'Never leave a friend behind. Friends are all we have to get us through this life-and they are the only things from this world that we could hope to see in the next.'
Dean Koontz

Is there someone from your past you have disconnected from? That you miss dearly? Someone who gets you or knows you like no other? Someone you wish you hadn't disconnected from? Reconnect with them, reminisce, laugh and share. Ring them, ZOOM with them or meet for a coffee. Take the time to bring them back into your life, don't be too busy for the ones you love.

51. TREAT YOURSELF

> 'Spend extravagantly on the things you love and cut costs mercilessly on the things you don't.'
> Ramit Sethi

Is there something you want but have talked yourself out of buying, is it a bit expensive, or you don't feel you deserve it, or it's a bit extravagant? Listen, if you can afford it, go on and treat yourself. I'm not saying do it every day, but you need to splurge and show the Universe that that is what you deserve, a life with blessings and beautiful things that make your heart sing. It could be a beautiful piece of jewellery or some shoes, a book collection, an instrument, some pretty dishes, or that gorgeous tree you want to plant in your garden. I recently took my kids to a fancy hotel by the ocean for two nights, this was extravagant for me, but I felt we deserved it and it let the Universe know, more of this please. Reward yourself, because you are amazing. You are of the Universe beautiful one.

52. SOLO DATE

> *'To love oneself is the beginning of a lifelong romance.'*
> Oscar Wilde

I covered this one when I asked you to step outside your comfort zone, but it's worth mentioning again as something to incorporate into your life on a regular basis. I used to dread the thought of going out by myself, wouldn't dream of sitting in café, or seeing a movie alone. I thought it made me look sad. Man was I wrong, I remember the first time I went to a double feature at the movies by myself. I was dating the usher at the cinema so I got in for free and watched two fabulous flicks all by myself, I was very young and it felt revolutionary. It makes me laugh, because I adore time by myself so much now. Now I love chilling in a cafe by myself, enjoying a coffee, maybe doing some writing, embracing the writer's cliché! But don't always feel the need to bury your face in your phone or a book, sometimes it's nice to just people watch. Take yourself out for a delicious meal. Pamper yourself you bloody awesome Queen!

53. BUY LINGERIE

> 'For me, wearing lingerie isn't about anyone else but me. If I dressed for others, I would be a miserable person.'
> Ashley Graham

Buy your sexy ass some goddess worthy lingerie. Not for anyone else but you! Wear it when you buy the groceries or take yourself out on a date night, remember it is FOR YOU. It doesn't matter what size or shape you are, we are all beautiful and you deserve to feel it. Lingerie companies are hearing this more and more. It's about time ALL bodies are celebrated, adored and respected. I struggle getting my size so I can only go to a local speciality store, but it is so worth it and you know if white granny undies and a comfy bra make you feel fine, get them! I wouldn't be caught dead in a G-string, so I get what I love to wear. So go get some and enjoy!

54. DRINK CEREMONIAL CACAO

> *'Cacao is not just a food, it's a superfood.'*
> David Wolfe

Each morning, when I am not swept away by the rush of making lunches and getting kids to school, arguing with my teen, feeding animals and cleaning up cat shit, I brew myself a yummy cup of ceremonial cacao. I brew it in my Thermomix with some cinnamon, honey, medicinal mushrooms and a plant-based milk, I then grab my journal and a smooth writing pen. I take a few deep breaths and just allow myself to stop and feel centered in time and space. Then I have a few sips of my cacao and begin writing, setting intentions and practising gratitude before really starting my day. Now, that sounds pretty wanky and it is, but cacao is a high vibe, delicious drink and coffee alternative, (not that I would ever give up my coffee) I love this little ceremony when I have the space to do it, it reconnects me with me and with spirit. There are lots of cacao ceremonies around as well, you might want to go along to one and feel your energy soar.

55. DREAM BIG

> 'The world only exists in your eyes.
> You can make it as big or as small as you can.'
> F. Scott Fitzgerald

Please stop putting limitations on yourself. Allow yourself the grace to dream of a beautiful life. Perhaps you dream of an illustrious film career, maybe you want to write a book, become a travel writer and tour the globe, create an empire, grow a mountain of food to share with your community? Whatever it is please don't let the dream go. A life without dreams is a dull life indeed. Journal it, vision board it, speak it, dream it and step into the glorious feelings that come with the big dreams as if they have already happened.

56. CULL YOUR CLOTHES

> *'Buy less, choose well.'*
> Vivienne Westwood

Stop holding onto clothes that make you feel frumpy, crappy, clothes that don't fit well, that have holes and tears. Get rid of the hyper colour t-shirt from the 80s (wait was that just me?) get rid of clothes that are too small, too big. Don't wait until you have lost the weight or done all the things you think you need to do before you can start dressing like the fucking Goddess you are.

DO IT NOW! You need to align with the vibe of things you want to attract. If the way you dress doesn't lift your spirits, it's time for an overhaul. Donate your old clothes or even better, have a swap party so everyone gets some new gear and clothes aren't wasted. Clothes with tears etc, if possible, use them as rags around the house. I've even turned old t-shirts into crop tops for my dog on slightly chilly days. Just dress so you feel confident, amazing and successful, because you are.

57. TURN OFF THE TV

> ❝
> *'If something got you to turn off T.V. it's a total success.'*
> Stephen King

Unless you are doing some Netflix and Chill, turn it off (Do people still say that?) Try and spend less time binge watching shows and a little more time living life. Now I love a good binge session, but I notice if I plant myself there for too long, my energy drains away and I become a lethargic, unmotivated blob. So, bring a little balance back, watch your favourite shows but break it up with things that stir up your energy, go for a walk, work on a project, dance, make a meal, go for coffee, anything that disrupts the binge watching energy slump.

58. CUT OUT MEAT AND DAIRY

> *'I think that most people don't really know the torture and murder that is the meat and dairy industry. And I think that we have a moral obligation to talk about it. And to expose it for what it really is. We are so indoctrinated with these images of happy animals on farms. On the covers of milk containers and all kinds of advertisements. And I think people need to know the truth. Those of us that have seen it for what it really is have an obligation to expose it.'*
> *Joaquin Phoenix*

Now I know not everyone is going to want to give this a go but there are so many benefits to making this switch. Not only will you feel better knowing you are not contributing to the death of billions of animals, you won't be ingesting all the crap they feed animals to keep them alive long enough and to grow fast enough to end up on your plate. Not to forget the terror and stress hormones surging through these sentient beings as they go to their deaths. Yuk. Even if none of that inspires you to give it a go, your body will thank you. A healthy, plant-based diet will clean up your body, your arteries, it'll sweep out all the crap, literally, you'll poop more AND dare I say give your soul a bit of a cleanse too. Not ingesting all that gross death will raise your vibe to the sky baby. There are SO many books, recipes and products available at your local supermarket to get you started. Why not give it a go?

59. SOUND HEALING

> ❝
>
> *'The Gong has the power of Creativity.*
> *Absolutely it is a therapy.*
> *And it can expand the mind beyond its horizon.'*
> Yogi Bhajan

Imagine laying somewhere comfy and warm and having beautiful healing sound waves washing over and through your body, this is sound healing. Sound healing is a beautiful way to envelope yourself with some healing vibes. There are so many recordings online you can listen too or if you're able, book yourself into a live sound healing and enjoy the raised energy all of those who attend. All you have to do is turn up, lay there and soak it in. If you're super keen, you could buy some crystal sound bowls and create your own healing vibes.

60. REIKI

> *'Reiki literally wakes up our divine essence so we can see our spirit behind the veils.'*
> Colleen Benelli

I asked my dear friend and Reiki Master, Julieanne Webster of Butterfly Therapies to tell us more about Reiki. "Reiki balances and aligns the energy in your body. Reiki is based on the idea that a life force energy flows within us and through us. It works on clearing out any energy blockages so they can be aligned and rebalanced. Reiki heals by flowing through the affected parts of the energy field and charging them with positive energy. It raises the vibrations of the energy field in and around the physical body where negative thoughts and feelings are attached. This causes the negative energy to break apart. In so doing, Reiki clears, straightens, heals and balances the energy pathways, thus allowing the life force to flow in a healthy and natural way. At the most basic level, everything has a vibrational frequency. We all feel and respond to each other's vibrations, even if we're not aware of it. When we operate at a higher frequency, we are healthier ~ less susceptible to disease and to the lower vibration emotions (sadness, fear, jealousy etc). Less likely to attract the negative energy of others. When you have a Reiki healing, you are pretty much giving your body a 'tune-up' honing in on any imbalances and blocks in the energy centres. So by lifting our vibration we can 'attract' anything we want into our life."

61. STOP PROCRASTINATING

> 'You cannot escape the responsibility of tomorrow by evading it today.'
> Abraham Lincoln

Whenever I have a back log of things I am avoiding, it drains my energy and stresses me out. Just like an app open in the background on your phone, it's in the back of your mind draining your battery with their incompleteness. Get them done, close them, get them out of the way, clear ALL the background apps, noise and clutter and clear your energy to bring in the good things. Then take a breath and congratulate yourself on getting shit done. You legend!

62. TAKE SOME RISKS

> *'Life is either a daring adventure or nothing at all.'*
> *Helen Keller*

'A life lived in fear is a life half lived,' this is my favourite quote from the film Strictly Ballroom. Don't make your life smaller because of fear. Take the chance, push yourself, as long as it isn't harming you or anyone else. You may be surprised how far you can go. Don't wait for the absence of fear, it is unlikely to come and as the very popular book by Susan Jeffers says, 'Feel the fear and do it anyway.' (An excellent read)

63. SIDE HUSTLE

> *'Determine never to be idle. No person will have occasion to complain of the want of time, who never loses any. It is wonderful how much may be done, if we are always doing.'*
> Thomas Jefferson

Having a side hustle is a brilliant way to cultivate your passions and bring in some extra dosh to relieve financial burden. It is a win-win. Maybe you've always wanted to make exquisite candles and sell them at your local market, maybe you have a lot of knowledge and can turn that into eBooks people need. Maybe you bake excellent dog treats or can knit fancy tea cosies? Whatever is your jam, turn it into a side hustle. Maybe you make jam! You've got this. Brainstorm all the things you are good at and see what come up with.

64. HUG

> 'Where I live if someone gives you a hug,
> it's from the heart.'
> Steve Irwin

I love a good hug, it's like a warm blanket of love enveloping you. Share some endorphins. Physical contact is so important for our mental wellbeing. Hug your parents, your kids, your partner, friends, fur babies, basically anyone that is open to sharing the love in a beautiful and respectful way. Get hugging and if you don't have enough souls to hug, book a regular massage and reap the benefits of physical touch (and happy muscles!)

65. ADOPT A RESCUE

> 'The greatness of a nation can be judged by the way its animals are treated.'
> Mahatma Gandhi

'Love the animals: God has given them the rudiments of thought and joy untroubled.'
Fyodor Dostoevsky

This one requires legitimate commitment, so only get an animal if you are one hundred percent committed to caring for it and giving it a brilliant life. The companionship of an animal is one of the most beautiful things in the world. But please, adopt don't shop. There are way too many animals needing homes in the world and way too many breeders. Just go to a local rescue shelter and see all the innocent beautiful souls wanting homes, apart from the heartbreak that you cannot adopt them all, you may just meet your furry soulmate.

66. LOOK AFTER MOTHER EARTH

> 'You carry Mother Earth within you. She is not outside of you. Mother Earth is not just your environment. In that insight of inter-being, it is possible to have real communication with the Earth, which is the highest form of prayer. In that kind of relationship, you have enough love, strength and awakening in order to change your life.'
> Thich Nhat Hanh

This planet is all we have and she's not happy. I know you are doing all the things, recycling, using less water, less power, eating more plants, less meat and dairy. How about volunteering for an organisation that helps our home? Bushcare? Clean up Australia, even craft groups that knit dishcloths reduce waste, breadmaking classes, although I'm sure you have perfected your sourdough through lockdowns. But you get the idea, do anything that reduces our impact on the earth. Write to MP's, follow causes, go to protests or just change small things in your daily life to tread lighter on the planet. There are so many ways you can help and make a difference, there really aren't any excuses now.

67. IGNORE THE HATER'S

> *'It's not your job to like me—it's mine.'*
> *Byron Katie*

It's not your business what others think of you. You can't control it, nor should you bother. Don't let other people control the way you live your life, you know not everyone is going to like you. Be kind, be compassionate, live by your values, stay in the light and let the darkness of people's judgement and criticism fade away. Don't return it, keep your vibe high. Be free. I remember once back in my 20's a woman in our social circle told me I was very opinionated. She wanted to hurt me, and I remember it shocked and shook me for a while. I didn't like not being liked or being judged and I felt inferior. Then I remembered that for a very long time, I didn't use my voice to express myself, I didn't think my opinions were valid. I didn't think anything I had to say had any value, so there was no way I was going to let someone's judgement of me shut me up again. I would continue to speak for myself but always with love as the motivation. I'm not always successful but I do my best. Know that when you put yourself 'out there' people won't like you, people will criticise you, it is just part of life. Do not let it make you small. You are enough as you are, live your best life, ignore the haters.

68. RELEASE YOUR EX

> *'You can spend minutes, hours, days, weeks, or even months over-analysing a situation; trying to put the pieces together, justifying what could've, would've happened... or you can just leave the pieces on the floor and move the fuck on.'*
> Tupac Shakur

> *'Girls you've gotta know when it's time to turn the page.'*
> Tori Amos

Here's a doozy. What are you hanging on for? They are an ex for a reason and while your energy is with them, it can't be with someone else. Go through your phone, go through your socials and cull. Get rid of the ex's number, no more drunk texting, no ringing when you feel a bit lonely, or when you're ovulating! If they were no good for you, let them go. No good will come over pining after someone no longer in your life. I know it's not easy sometimes to let people go, I've chosen to break up with people and sometimes still miss them and think of them often, but I know having them in my life is no good for me (or them for that matter) So delete and move on sweetness.

69. NO STALKING

> 'Women never stalk men; they just research them intensely.'
> Matshona Dhliawayo

Part of letting them go is this. Don't stalk your ex! I repeat, do not stalk your ex. It serves no purpose but to make you miserable. It is a big pile of gross energy you don't need. Whether you are grateful they are out of your life or wish you had them back, stalking them will only bring up old gunk. Block them, delete them, move on, work on your beautiful self, if it is meant to be it will. Come on Goddess, you deserve better. Who cares what they are doing now, or who they are with. Thank god they aren't with you making your life a misery anymore. You focus on you and let them go baby go. Or else it will drain you of your joy and we do not want that.

70. MIRROR WORK

> *'Look in the mirror and tell yourself how wonderful you are.'*
> Louise Hay

This can be confronting, I admit. But it is also a technique that can powerfully shift your love and respect for yourself. If you don't honour yourself, why would anyone else? Stand in front of the mirror, naked if you can and say all the things you love about yourself. I love my eyes, I love my thighs, my stomach, whatever it is. Love the parts of you that you feel insecure about, it's just you and the mirror. Talk to the inner you, tell yourself you are proud of you, you respect and honour and will care for you, you love you. You might cry but that's ok, you are healing and releasing. Be brave. You are worth it.

71. TRAVEL

> 'Once the travel bug bites there is no known antidote, and I know that I shall be happily infected until the end of my life.'
> Michael Palin

Now the world has opened up, get out and explore, explore your own country, explore other countries, learn about other cultures. See how big the world really is and how EVERYONE has their own shit going on. Go on a road trip somewhere you love, jump in a new ocean, walk a new path, climb the Eiffel Tower, run through an English meadow. Go to a town near you that you never explore, it doesn't have to be expensive or big. You get the idea, and if you can't afford to do that, catch a train or bus somewhere new.

72. BE PRESENT

> *'As soon as you honor the present moment, all unhappiness and struggle dissolve, and life begins to flow with joy and ease. When you act out the present-moment awareness, whatever you do becomes imbued with a sense of quality, care, and love – even the most simple action.'*
> Eckhart Tolle

Stop rushing through your life, stop and notice your surroundings, smell the damn flowers, sit down to eat, notice how it tastes. Notice how your body feels, how the air feels against your skin, how you feel after that hug. Don't disappear into Netflix, don't numb yourself out of your own life. I went through a period in lockdown when I couldn't bear to deal with the thoughts in my head, the things I needed to do, I was feeling low and depressed. I started binge watching The Kardashians, I'd never watched it prior, except for catching it occasionally on TV, but I put in some serious hours watching them live THEIR lives, admiring their beautiful homes, wishing I had some of that, I became so absorbed that I forgot about my own life. I stopped doing anything because it was easier to escape. Then one day I went outside, the sun was finally shining, the air was warm, and I played in my garden and finally snapped out if it. I wanted to be in my life, wanted to make my home pretty, focus more on my kids, my health, my creative work. The pull to disappear lessened the more space I gave myself from the screen and the more attention I paid to my life and to slowing it down. I gardened mindfully, ate my meals mindfully and played with the kids mindfully.

73. GRATITUDE

> "
>
> *'The first step toward discarding a scarcity mentality involves giving thanks for everything that you have.'*
> *'The Universe provides abundantly when you're in a state of gratefulness.'*
> Wayne Dyer

Gratitude is a big one. Everyone seems to be talking about being grateful, and with good reason. If you want to bring more goodness into your life, you need to align your energy with what you love, with the good ALREADY in your life. If you focus on what you don't like, guess what you'll get? More of what you don't like. You've heard it a million times, now it's time to commit to doing it, every morning and/or night write down 5-10 things you are grateful for. I also like to write down things I am grateful for before I even have them, as if I have them, for example, I am grateful for my new car, my soul mate, my dream home, my awesome career, whatever it is, be grateful!

74. GET A MENTOR

> 'The delicate balance of mentoring someone is not creating them in your own image, but giving them the opportunity to create themselves.'
> Steven Spielberg

Find a mentor or a coach that you align with. If you are struggling to stay on track or to even get going, having someone to help guide you, to keep you accountable and to offer stellar advice can be worth the investment. As long as you connect with the person you choose, and feel inspired and motivated, you are good to go. I have a health coach at the moment, not because I am fancy and rich, far bloody from it but I really struggle with eating well and looking after myself because I allow myself to get overwhelmed by life. She is my cheerleader, she helps me do the hard things and to put down the crap and take in the good. Perhaps you have a good friend with similar goals to you, be each other's cheerleaders, at least then it is free.

75. DEFINE YOUR VALUES

> *'Open your arms to change but don't let go of your values.'*
> Dalai Lama

> *'Values are like fingerprints. Nobodies are the same but you leave them all over everything you do.'*
> Elvis Presley

Do you have a clear idea of what your values are? And if so, do you live by them? Do you make decisions based on your values? Staying in alignment with who you really are and what matters to you is healing and maintains your integrity. I know if I choose to do something that isn't in alignment with my values, it makes me feel off centre and gunky. But if you stay in the light and honour the true you, your vibration is celebrating. Sit down with a nice cup of tea and think about what is important to you, what do you value in life? in people? How do you want to live your life? How do you want to be remembered? Write it all down and then see if you are doing so.

76. DON'T BE A DOORMAT

> 'Don't want to wink at nobody, don't want to be <u>winked</u> at Don't want to be used by <u>nobody</u> for a doormat Don't want to <u>confuse</u> nobody, don't want to be confused Don't want to <u>amuse</u> nobody, don't want to be amused.'
> Bob Dylan

> 'You're either a Goddess or a doormat.'
> Pablo Picasso

You are worthy. You are worthy. You are worthy. Get it? You are a Rockstar, don't let anybody walk all over you. Shine bright. That is all.

77. SAY NO

> 'You have to decide what your highest priorities are and have the courage pleasantly, smilingly, and non-apologetically ~ to say no to other things. And the way to do that is by having a bigger yes burning inside.'
> Stephen Covey

> 'Freedom comes when you learn to let go, creation comes when you learn to say no.'
> Madonna

Don't overcommit to things if you can help it, don't say yes if you'd rather pull your own teeth out than go. Turn off your phone, have some quiet time, if they can't reach you they can't ask! But most of all, learn how to say no to things that drain you and don't align with your highest self. Set and maintain your boundaries. Learn when to say no ~ your energy is precious, you need to take care of it.

78. SMILE

> 'Don't cry because it's over. Smile because it happened.'
> Dr Seuss
>
> 'Let my soul smile through my heart and my heart smile though my eyes, that I may scatter rich smiles in sad hearts.'
> Paramahansa Yogananda

Planting a smile on your dial can help increase the release of serotonin and dopamine which makes you feel good. Even if you feel crappola, smiling can 'trick' your brain into thinking you are Happy as Larry, and the old 'fake it till you make it' comes into play. It's a little trick to help boost mood and raise your vibe. I'm not saying walk around with a deranged smile on your face making everyone think you have been cast as the next Joker, but try it out, a little smile here and there. Still honour your moods, but see if it makes a difference for you? Can't hurt!

79. VISUALISATION

> *'Visualize the most amazing life imaginable to you. Close your eyes and see it clearly. Then hold the vision for as long as you can. Now place the vision in God's hands and consider it done.'*
> Marianne Williamson

A vital part of manifesting is visualisation. Set aside a few minutes each day to visualise yourself having achieved a certain goal or simply living the life you desire - smell it, hear it, feel it. Feel the joy of having received all that your heart desires. Embrace that joy, smile, dance, laugh, be ecstatic. All of this will ramp up the manifesting power and will let the Universe know exactly what you want. You don't need to do this for long, 3-5 minutes a day is all you need, most importantly is how you feel in those 3-5 minutes. Better to feel the joy for 3 minutes than to sit in a lacklustre visualisation for 20 minutes.

80. LOVE YOURSELF

> 'The most terrifying thing is to accept oneself completely.'
> C.G. Jung

> 'If you have the ability to love, love yourself first.'
> Charles Bukowski

If you don't love yourself, who will? You got to put your mask on first, fill yourself up with love and acceptance and forgiveness. Then and only then can you truly give out into the world. Then you will attract someone worthy of you. Even if you already have a loving partner or are happy flying through the world solo, loving yourself is a pre-requisite to happiness. It can take time and commitment to really embrace this for some. Add more and more self-love and kind words and you will eventually squeeze out most of the negativity that makes you feel less than. It's like when you change your diet for the better, keep adding more and more healthy delicious foods (self-love) and it will eventually crowd out the junk. You deserve this.

81. TALK TO A STRANGER

> 'There are no strangers in here, just friends you haven't meet.'
> Roald Dahl

This goes hand in hand with stepping outside your comfort zone, most of us travel through the world with our eyes cast down to avoid connecting with people we don't know. How about making eye contact and having a conversation with someone new? You could be waiting in line at the supermarket, at an art exhibition, waiting for your take away coffee. I've had awesome conversations with people when I have nothing to do but wait. Not everyone will be willing, but you can gauge this pretty quickly. You never know who you might connect with and if they think you are a little kooky, that's fun too!

82. MAKE THE FIRST MOVE

> *'I'm finally dating. It's fun.'*
> Kristin Chenoweth

Are you sitting there waiting for him/her/they to ask you out? Take a chance, make the first move. Look, if they say no, at least you know and wont waste another second waiting for them. This can be scary, I know and not everyone's cup of tea but maybe it's something you can try at least once in life? Be brave, be confident, fake it till you make it, shake it up. Release old patriarchal ideologies, there are no rules.

83. COMMUNITY

❝

'What should young people do with their lives today? Many things, obviously. But the most daring thing is to create stable communities in which the terrible disease of loneliness can be cured.'
Kurt Vonnegut

Everybody needs community, everybody needs connection, the right people and the right connections that is. Surround yourself with high vibe, happy, caring people and feel your energy lift. Remove negative people from your circle, send them away with love. Connect with people who inspire and support you and who you can inspire and support. Find groups with the same interests as you. Maybe it's a book club, a wine appreciation club, a running group, a Star Wars fan club, who knows? Go along, join in and connect baby!

84. HONESTY

> 'Be honest with yourself. The world is not honest with you. The world loves hypocrisy. When you are honest with yourself you find the road to inner peace.'
> Paramahansa Yogananda

Time to stop and take stock. Are you living the life you desire? Are you making excuses as to why you can't get that job, get healthier, meet new people, follow your dreams? Are you sabotaging yourself? I know how that goes, I'm excellent at it. It's time to be honest with yourself and figure out what if anything is holding you back? Fear, low self-esteem? Get a counsellor, psychologist, healer, coach, mentor, whatever it takes to work through and release some of those nasty old beliefs we cling too that stop us reaching our full potential. And no more excuses, be honest with yourself about where you are at and where you want to be and work towards it.

85. HAVE FAITH

> *'Faith is taking the first step when you don't see the whole staircase.'*
> Martin Luther King, Jr

> *'Faith gives you an inner strength and a of balance and perspective in life.'*
> Gregory Peck

Have faith that what you are manifesting is coming your way, trust the Universe has your back, trust you are being cared for. This doesn't mean you sit back and do nothing, you do the work but trust it is a co-creating deal between you and the Universe. Have faith there is something much bigger than your daily grind that is working magic behind the scenes for you. When you have faith, it is easier to relax, surrender and to let go. Grasping won't help, obsessing won't help, but having faith will.

86. GET HEALTHY

'It is health that is real wealth and not pieces of gold and silver.'
Mahatma Gandhi

'To keep the body in good health is a duty...otherwise we shall not be able to keep our mind strong and clear.'
Buddha

Get your health in check, do what you need to do to have your body, mind and spirit in optimum condition. The better you feel, the higher your energy, the more co-creating magic. Book in to see a Naturopath, Homeopath, Integrative Dr, Chiropractor, Osteopath. Just get it done. Go to the dentist, I know you've been putting it off, get your skin checked, have the colonoscopy. Look after your body, it's the only one you have. Just like you service your car and give it premium fuel, do the same for you. Premium food, premium thoughts, premium vibes.

87. SUPPLEMENTS

> *'I treat myself pretty good. I take lots of vacations, I eat well, I take supplements... I get plenty of sleep, I drink plenty of water and I stayaway from drama and stress.'*
> Reba McEntire

Taking some chosen supplements is a wonderful way to complement a healthy diet and lifestyle to achieve optimum health and high vibration. Best to see a Naturopath or Integrative Dr and have some bloods done, then you know exactly what you may need to optimise your health that you aren't getting from your nutrition. If you eat super healthy you probably won't need much, but if you do, buy good quality, professionally recommended supplements and take the appropriate dose as advised.

88. INFRARED SAUNA

> *'The sauna is a poor man's pharmacy.'*
> Unknown

Go Infrared! Detox baby. Sweat out all the nasties. Close your eyes and do a meditation while you sit there letting the sauna and your body do its work and keep hydrated with lots of water. An infrared sauna is different to a traditional steam sauna, the infrared heat penetrates your body relaxing you and helping to get the nasties out and you don't have to sit in one with a bunch of sweaty dudes in towels, unless you want too! Soothing and glorious.

89. HYDRATE

> 'Pure water is the world's first and foremost medicine.'
> Slovakian Proverb

We are mostly water, if you are dehydrated nothing is going to work right. We literally drop dead if we don't get enough water. I feel awful if not properly hydrated and get lots of headaches. One of my favourite psychic mediums is always telling people to drink more water. It cleans your body up and helps clear your energy. It makes your skin look lush too. Grab a bottle that keeps you accountable, I use one that has markers to help me make sure I am drinking enough. Get a good water filter for home and fill up your reusable water bottle when you go out, let's not buy any plastic water bottles. If plain water bores you, add some lemon or lime and drink up.

90. POOP REGULARLY

> *'Just be ordinary and nothing special. Eat your food, move your bowels, pass water, and when you're tired, go and lie down. The ignorant will laugh at me, but the wise will understand.'*
> Bruce Lee

Why am I talking about poop? Does this help raise your vibe? Well if you are clogged up and full of waste, you're not going to be feeling that awesome and your energy will be stagnant. Plus, if you strain away, you'll get hemmy's and they SUCK. Get some fibre in you and as I keep stressing, lots of water and poop away! Plus, it's excellent for your overall health. Add flaxseeds or chia to your diet, read 'Fibre Fuelled,' by Dr Will Bulsiewicz and get pooping.

91. EAT YOUR GREENS

> *'There's a great metaphor that one of my doctors uses: If a fish is swimming in a dirty tank and gets sick, do you take it to the vet and amputate the fin? No, you clean the water. So, I cleaned up my system. By eating organic raw greens, nuts and healthy fats, I am flooding my body with enzymes, vitamins and oxygen.'*
> *Kris Carr*

This is not new information so if you love them chow down, if not find ones you can tolerate and get them into you, chuck them in a smoothie so you can't taste them. Green vegetables and leafy greens are one of the healthiest foods on the planet, we need lots of them, so no more excuses. Make stir-frys, salads, roast veg and greens, more smoothies. Get them into your body several times a day. At the very least, get a high-quality green powder you can add to some water daily. Go green!

92. NEVER GIVE UP

'Never give up. You only get one life. Go for it.'
Richard E. Grant

You may change your mind about what you want in life as time goes by, I have many times, but never give up on yourself. I am not saying every dream will come true, but if you give up then it sure as hell wont. Have some faith, have a lot of faith, keep on swimming, keep on dreaming. Sit down and write out your goals, your desires, are you still in alignment with them all? Cull what isn't for you anymore and surge forth with the rest.

93. ADD PLANTS

> 'To plant a garden is to believe in tomorrow.'
> Audrey Hepburn

Fill your home with nature. Use lush green plants, spunky little succulents or some cheeky ferns to greenify your space. Having greenery in your home is calming, soothing and helps keep your air nice and clean. Look after them, talk to them and watch them thrive. If you kill everything green, get some spiky little cactus and let them sit happily in a sunny spot. There is a plant for everyone, do a bit of research and see what appeals then bring it home and create some Zen.

94. INSPIRED ACTION

> *'Don't overthink the process of creation. It doesn't matter how your goals manifest. Believe they will and take inspired action.*
> *The Universe will make it happen.'*
> *Vex King*

It doesn't matter how many visions boards you make, how many affirmations you say or intentions you set. If you then sit on the couch watching reruns of The Office, waiting for everything to appear, you'll be waiting a LONG bloody time. You need to meet the Universe part way and put in some effort. You need to take baby steps or action steps towards your goals and dreams often whilst doing all the other stuff too. THEN the Universe can help bring what you desire to you. You won't be a famous author is you never write a word, you won't have a healthy body if you gorge on donuts every day, you won't land your dream job if you don't send out resumes and upgrade your skills, you won't win the lotto if you never buy a ticket, you get the drift...

95. YOGA

> 'Yoga does not just change the way we see things, it transforms the person who sees.'
> B.K.S Iyengar

Stretch it out. You know this is good for you. I am probably one of the most inflexible people in the world so my favourite pose is Childs Pose, where basically you sit like a frog and chill, but that said, I find yoga to be as beneficial as it is challenging. It is calming, centering, and wonderful for your body. There are so many kinds and I am no expert but do some research and find a style that works for you. Be it Hatha, Yin or some sweaty Bikram. There are cool online programs as I mentioned my favourite is Yoga with Adrienne.

96. SAGE YOUR HOME

> *'If you don't want to come to my house when I burn sage, that means the sage is working.'*
> *Unknown*

Clean that negative energy out! Get rid of all the bad juju, make space for the positive, life affirming energy to come rushing in. Throw open the doors and windows, light up and get that juicy smoke into all corners and cupboards and say some clearing affirmations as you go. 'Out with the bad juju, in with all the good vibes!' I do this regularly, especially after someone has been in my home that makes things feel a little off. But also, just whenever I feel the energy needs a refresh. You can also use Palo Santo if you like, or both!

97. FULL AND NEW MOON RITUALS

> *'Go slowly, my lovely moon, go slowly.'*
> Khaled Hosseini

Each new and full moon is a wonderful opportunity to release things that no longer serve you and to set intentions. Doing a meditation, ritual and some journaling is the perfect way to celebrate, you can find new moon and full moon meditations on meditation apps and You Tube. Mine are on You Tube and Insight Timer. The full moon is a time to release and the new moon is a great time to set intentions. Writing down and burning a list of all things you want to release is fun and for setting intentions, get out your favourite journal and speak to the Universe. It is magic time. Pop your crystals outside to cleanse and charge under a full moon too and if you are super woo-woo like me, put some filtered water out under a full moon in a glass bottle or container and make Moon Water, then bathe in it, drink it, water your plants with it, whatever you like. Enjoy the beautiful moon energy in every way you can.

98. EAT CARBS

> 'Spaghetti can be eaten most successfully if you inhale it like a vacuum cleaner.'
> Sophia Loren

Carbs are not the enemy. They are not going to kill you. Or more to the point, just don't follow fad diets, they have been proven to not work. Instead focus on eating healthy wholefoods, organic when possible. Get rid of processed crap, get rid of foods that make you feel like shit. Eat the rainbow of colours, be mindful when you eat, do the best you can with what you have. But allow yourself some delicious pasta and other carby treats, life's too short not too.

99. FORGET YOUR AGE

> 'Age is just a number. It's totally irrelevant unless, of course, you happen to be a bottle of wine.'
> Joan Collins

Don't let 'being too young' or 'being too old' stop you from pursuing your dreams. Time is made up, you are ageless. Go for it! I reformed my rock band after nearly 20 years at the age of 48, I launched a new business at 49, I am writing my first book now at 50. If I thought I was too old, I'd still be sitting on the couch watching Schitt's Creek. Who am I kidding, I can't stop watching Schitt's Creek. The point is you are never too old to pursue your dreams, I don't want you to live with regrets, please keep going. If your 60 and want to go back to school, do it! If your 15 and want to start a business, do it now. Give yourself permission to let go of any and all of society's bullshit rules and get out there, you're worth it.

100. CUT CORDS

> ❝
>
> *'I take back my power by cutting energy cords that have formed between myself and any person, situation, or thing that no longer serves me.'*
> Unknown

People come and go from our lives all the time, and most often we are still connected to many of them energetically. Same with events, traumas and things. This can be very draining, and it is best to cut the cords with these people to free up our energy (and theirs) and to send them on their way. Cut the energetic cords that bond you to things that weigh you down and keep you frozen in the past. A simple meditation/visualisation is all it takes, there are loads available for free, try the app Insight Timer and find on that works for you. Maybe find one with Archangel Michael, he uses his sword to cut them away.

101. EARTHING

> 'The grass is soft! It's cool! I feel free! Running around in the grass in your bare feet can be very exciting...'
> Charles M. Schulz

> 'We touch the earth with our feet, and we heal the earth, we heal ourselves...'
> Thich Nhat Hanh

Earthing is also known as grounding. What does it do? Basically, when you pop your bare feet on the earth, your body takes up free electrons (natures antioxidants) and lots of healing and yummy good stuff takes place. How's that for science talk? You may benefit from improved sleep, reduced inflammation, pain reduction, and lots more. Take off your shoes and get your beautiful feet on the earth, you can also buy earthing sheets for your bed and earthing mats to put your feet on while you sit at a computer, there are many options about. Have a read of Clinton Ober's book 'Earthing,' if you're interested in exploring this more and get grounded. Just watch out for bees in the clover, learnt that one the hard way...

102. MANDALAS

> "Each person's life is like a mandala – a vast, limitless circle. We stand in the centre of our own circle, and everything we see, hear and think forms the mandala of our life."
> — Pema Chödrön

Mandala's are a brilliant way to tap into your creativity and to use meditation creatively. There is a quiet space you enter into when you focus solely on colouring and even drawing your own Mandalas. Not all meditation needs to be sitting crossed legged on your zafu! Plus, it's fun and kids love doing it too. So, grab some beautiful colourful pencils and have at it. I like sticking mine to book covers, in particular 'My Dream Life' scrapbook. If you don't want to draw one, do a google search for 'mandalas' and choose some you love and print them out. There are so many beautiful designs online, or you can buy a mandala colouring book.

103. SEE A PSYCHIC MEDIUM

> *'I shall not commit the fashionable stupidity of regarding everything I cannot explain as a fraud.'*
> Carl Jung

I have to confess, I am a medium junkie. I have always been fascinated with all things metaphysical and love connecting with the other side using a reputable psychic medium. If you need some clarity, some direction or wish to communicate with some loved ones who have passed then this is a wonderful option. For me it is a brilliant way to connect with my parents who have both passed and also get some well needed life guidance. Find someone highly recommended. Positive word of mouth and reviews are a great way to filter out the fakers. And also consider there are many types, a psychic is not necessarily a medium, some only use tarot, some channel, it is a wonderful world to explore. Just choose your person wisely.

104. ESSENTIAL OILS

> *'Self-care is an essential part of a healthy life. Essential oils figure in many at-home remedies to smooth the skin, soothe the spirit, and calm the mind.'*
> Amy Leigh Mercree

I'm not selling oils, in fact I only own a few but adding a couple of drops to your bath, body and even food and drink can be beneficial. Always check they are safe for consumption or for putting on your skin. Get a beautiful oil diffuser and fill your home with scrumptious healing scents. I personally love some Ylang Ylang in my bath, and you will find what works for you. They can be added to little rollers, you can put some drops on a handkerchief, a small spray bottle, there are some many options. I stayed at a fancy hotel recently and they had a small lavender essential oil spray bottle for your pillows, divine. But only buy top quality stuff, otherwise you are wasting your dosh.

105. BREATHWORK

> *'Just breathe and reclaim your soul.'*
> *Wim Hof*

Primarily stemming from ancient yogic traditions, breathwork is a wonderful way to reduce stress, improve vitality which will in turn raise your vibration. Perhaps you have already experienced it at a yoga class? There are breathwork practitioners and loads online to get you started. Even just placing your hands on your stomach and chest and noticing the rise and fall as you inhale and exhale is a great start. It is calming, invigorating and great for your nervous system.

106. SWIM IN THE OCEAN

> 'Live in the sunshine, swim the sea, drink the wild air.'
> Ralph Waldo Emerson

A dip in the ocean is a beautiful way of connecting with nature, cleansing your body, mind and soul. Feeling the awesome power of mother nature as she pushes and pulls you about. Feel the salt on your skin, cleansing and healing, it is a great way to refresh yourself. Sit on the beach and listen to the waves, close your eyes and be grateful, take some deep breaths and release the tension from your body. If you have a pooch, take them for a sunset walk along the shore. Watch the sunset with a loved one, let the waves wash over your feet. If you are lucky enough to live by the sea, don't waste it.

107. PROTEST

> 'He who passively accepts evil is as much involved in it as he who helps to perpetrate it. He who accepts evil without protecting against it is really cooperating with it.'
> Martin Luther King, Jr.

> 'There are good reasons for being in jail – for protesting.'
> Tracy Chapman

Standing up for something you believe in is soul affirming, invigorating and powerful. Whether you are marching the streets in a peaceful protest, painting banners and striking for climate change or standing up for the animals still used and abused in circuses and in labs. Use your voice to create change. Perhaps your forte is letter writing, collecting signatures, public speaking? Whatever it is, do it. We need more people to give a shit, more people to take action to create positive change in the world, let's not leave a big pile of shit for our kids to clean up.

108. VISIT A SANCTUARY OR TEMPLE

> *'Sanctuaries are magical places – dare I say holy?'*
> Colleen Patrick-Goudreau

Going to an animal sanctuary is without a doubt one of my favourite things to do in the world. Connecting with the animals, seeing them happy, hearing their stories, seeing first-hand the good in the world fills my heart with love. Supporting sanctuaries with a one off or regular donation is even better. Or maybe a temple is more your vibe? I love going to the Buddhist Temple in Wollongong, near Sydney. I have a delicious vegetarian lunch and then wander around the gardens. Be respectful and observe the customs of any place you visit. They also usually offer meditation courses, so check them out.

109. TEA TIME

> *'Drink your tea slowly and reverently, as if it is the axis on which the world earth revolves ~ slowly, evenly, without rushing toward the future.'*
> *Thich Nhat Hanh*

Stop everything and brew yourself a delicious cup of tea, the act of being mindful whilst preparing your tea is a meditation in itself. Once your tea is brewed and delicious, made just to your liking, sit, relax and with each sip, think about things you are grateful for, people you love, things that bring you joy. Focus on being present with your breath and if you are feeling extra nurturing, dunk your favourite bikkie in and enjoy.

110. FOREST BATHING

'In the forest, there's no need to try to relax. Just go outside and Nature will work her magic to relax and restore you. Studies show that people feel more relaxed after just fifteen minutes of being in nature. And they report feeling greater vitality, too. Being surrounded by aliveness literally makes us feel more alive.'
Julia Plevin

Made popular in Japan, simply put, forest bathing is to find a suitable place where you can do a gentle walk and that has places to sit. As you slowly walk, notice and listen to everything, including your own body and senses, really connect to and absorb your environment. Choose a lovely place to sit for at least 20 minutes before giving thanks and acknowledging the gifts you receive from the forest. To me, it is a beautiful meditation and healing time and well worth a try. Plus it's free!

111. SURRENDER

> *'Always say "yes" to the present moment. What could be more futile, more insane, than to create inner resistance to what already is? what could be more insane than to oppose life itself, which is now and always now? Surrender to what is. Say "yes" to life — and see how life suddenly starts working for you rather than against you.'*
> Eckhart Tolle

Now it is time to simply let go and to surrender. Trying to control everything, to 'grasp' is exhausting and quite simply impossible. Trust that the Universe has your back, that if you are following your intuition, you are on the right path and that things will unfold in the right time for you. How freeing is it to say, 'Hey Universe! I'm handing it all over to you now. All the stress, the worry, the grasping, the clinging, I know you have my back and I surrender.' Then you have the time and space to follow your dreams, to do all the things that make you feel good and to focus on having a wonderful life. Take a deep breath and when you exhale imagine all of the heaviness, the burden draining away from your body. Feel the lightness now. Do this a few times. Go back to your mirror work, look deeply into your eyes and say 'I Surrender' and have a joyous, amazing life. I love you.

NOTES

NOTES

NOTES

THANK YOU FOR READING.

Find me here:
www.elizabethbowie.au

ACKNOWLEDGEMENTS

My biggest thank you goes to my children Jasper and Harper who give me moments of peace so I can type my words, who give me so much love and hugs when most needed. Who give me a reason to strive for the best for them and for me. I adore you two! To my menagerie, what would life be without you? Dull indeed. To my bestie Kirstie, who has always encouraged me and believed in me when many haven't. Set up the beach chairs, pour the margarita's, I am on my way. Finally, to you dear reader, thank you for reading my words, thank you for buying this little book, thank you for being you.

Peace.

www.ingramcontent.com/pod-product-compliance
Lightning Source LLC
Chambersburg PA
CBHW072059110526
44590CB00018B/3242